I0528533

SPHere

soverelgnty

Abraham Kuyper

Monergism Books

Copyright © 2024

Sphere Sovereignty by Abraham Kuyper

Translated by George Kamp

Published by by Monergism Books
P.O. Box 491
West Linn Oregon 97068
www.monergism.com

All rights reserved.

No portion of this book may be reproduced in any form without written permission
from the publisher or author, except as permitted by U.S. copyright law.

ISBN: 978-1-961807-66-2

contents

Introduction

The men upon whom rests the administration of this Institution assigned to me the honor of inaugurating their school for higher education by introducing it to the authorities and the people. In so doing, I ask that you grant me an unstinted measure of benevolent listening and charitable judgment. A request, the earnestness of which will be evident if you consider that I am not to deliver an inaugural oration nor a rectoral discourse, but that, barred from the quiet hiding-place of scientific research, the nature of my task drives me to that treacherous terrain of public life, where nettles and thorns on all hedges burn and wound at every step. Indeed, we cannot conceal, nor would any of us disguise the fact that we were not urged to this task, like Maecenases, because of love for the abstract sciences; the urge to this risky, if not presumptuous endeavor was the deep-grained sense of duty, which impressed upon us that what we were doing must be done, for Christ's sake, for the Lord's

Name, because of a high and holy importance for our people and our land. Thus our action was not at all ingenious; we are thoroughly convinced that the interest which, amid favorable and adverse rumors, anticipated this Institution's founding and now attends it at its opening, is not in any sense related to our persons, but proceeded exclusively from the public's impression that the Netherlands were witnessing an event that might well leave its traces in the future of the nation. For, if a higher criterion could have induced us to acquiesce in the existing conditions, why would we have undertaken this task? Most mildly stated, our undertaking implies a protest against the present environment and a suggestion that something better is available and even that consideration causes a certain embarrassment and diffidence, if only because of the semblance of presumption which follows it like a shadow. This could cause offense; this could hurt; there- fore I hasten to assure you that (whether we look at the might of learning, influence, and gold which oppose us, or whether we humbly consider our own importance and smallness), no lofty conceit but a quiet humility is expressed in the assurance of our words. We should have preferred to remain in the background; it would have been much more comfortable to see others taking the lead. However, since this could not be, since we must act, we came to the forefront, indeed not indifferent to men's favor of aversion, but ordering our line of conduct exclusively in accordance with the demands of the criterion of God's honor.

You are now waiting for me to tell you what this school which we are introducing expects to accomplish in the life of the Netherlands; why it brandishes the liberty cap on the tip of its lance; and why it peers so intently at the book of Reformed religion. Permit me to link up the answer to those three questions engendered by the one concept of "Sphere Sovereignty" by pointing to this Sphere Sovereignty as the hallmark of our institution

in its national significance,

in its scientific purpose, and

in its Reformed character.

I. SPHere sovereignty's national significance

T he first part of my discourse then will be to present our Institution in its national significance. The life of our nation, too, is also engaged in struggling through a crisis in this awesome century, a crisis which is experienced in common with all involved nations, a crisis which pervades all of reflective humanity. Every crisis affects a life, and during the process of illness either promises a renewal of youth or threatens destruction by death. Now I ask, what is the affected life in this case? What is at stake in this crisis, also for our nation? And who would repeat the answer of former times, as if the struggle were concerned with progress or preservation; with one-sidedness or versatility; with ideal or reality; or with rich or poor? The inadequacy, the disproportion, the shallowness of each of these diagnoses is too apparent to do so. "Clerical" and "liberal" then became the watchword, as if it were a question of misuse or purification of spiritual influence. Finally this screen was also contemptuously overturned, and from the center to a constantly widening circle the realization penetrated -- a realization which originally was understood only by the leading prophets of our century -- that in the present world crisis we are not concerned with nuances, with interests, or with justice, but with a living person, with Him who once swore that He was a King, and Who, because of that Sovereign King-pretension gave His life on the cross on Golgotha.

"The Nazarene our holy inspirer; inspiring ideal; ideal genius of piety!" has long been the candid cry; but history has challenged that praise as being a contradiction of the Nazarene's own claim. Nothing less than Messiah, Anointed therefore Sovereign of all kings, and 'possessing all power in heaven and on earth', was the pronouncement of his calm and clear god-man consciousness. Not a hero of faith, not a martyr, but King of the Jews, that is, Bearer of the Sovereignty; this was inscribed upon His cross, as a criminal presumption, which demanded his death. And because of that Sovereignty, because of the existence or non-existence of that power of the One born of Mary, the spirits that think, the powers that rule, and the nations that participate are as turbulent now as they were in the first three centuries. That King of the Jews, the saving truth to which all peoples respond with AMEN, or, the principial lie, which all peoples ought to oppose, that is the problem of Sovereignty which, even as it was once presented in the blood of the

Nazarene, has again rent apart the world of our spiritual, our human, our national existence.

What is Sovereignty? Do you not agree with me when I describe it as: the authority that has the right and the duty to exercise power to break all resistance to its will and to avenge such resistance? And does not that ineradicable national sense come to expression in you that the original, absolute Sovereignty cannot rest in any creature but must coincide with God's Majesty? If you believe in Him as Planner and Creator, as Establisher and Determiner of all things, your soul must also proclaim the Triune God as the only and absolute Sovereign. Provided, and this I would stress, that one also acknowledges that this exalted Sovereign delegated and does delegate His authority to human beings; so that on earth one actually does not meet God Himself in things visible, but that sovereign authority is always exercised through an office held by men.

And in that assigning of God's Sovereignty to an office held by man the extremely important question arises: how does that delegation of authority work? Is that all-embracing Sovereignty of God delegated undivided to one single man; or does an earthly Sovereign possess the power to compel obedience only in a limited circle; a circle bordered by other circles in which another is Sovereign?

The answers to this question will vary, depending upon whether one is within the sphere of Revelation or outside of it.

For of old the answer to that question by those in whose world of thought there was no room for a special revelation has always been: "insofar as feasible undivided, but penetrating all circles." "Insofar as feasible", for God's Sovereignty over that which is above is outside of man's reach; His Sovereignty over nature is outside of man's power; His Sovereignty over destiny is outside of man's disposal. But for the rest, yes, without "Sphere Sovereignty", the state's unlimited rule; disposing of persons, their life, their rights, their conscience, and even their faith. It was then many gods, and therefore, because of the *vis unita fortior* [strength united is stronger], the one unlimited State was more imposing, more majestic than the divided might of the gods. And because of this the State, embodied in Caesar, itself became God. The god-State which could not tolerate any other gods beside itself. Thus came the passion for world-dominion. Divus Augustus! [divine Augustus] with Caesarism as the worship service. A profoundly sinful idea, which was not analyzed until eighteen centuries later, also for thinking minds, in [Georg Wilhelm Friedrich] Hegel's system of the State as "den gegenwärtigen Gott" [the current God].

On the other hand, "not insofar as feasible, but in the absolute sense this Sovereignty is to be delegated undivided and unbroken!" This is Jehovah's declaration to Israel through the medium of the interpreters of Messianic prophecy. And that man-Messiah made His appearance, with power in heaven; with power over nature; with the pretension of power over all people; with power, in all people, also over conscience, also over faith; even the ties between mother and child must give way when He demanded obedience. Here then is absolute Sovereignty; dominating all visible and invisible things; all that is both spiritual and material; all placed in the hands of one man. Not one of the kingdoms, but the absolute Kingdom. "To be King, for that purpose I was born, and for that purpose I came into the world." "All power in heaven and on earth is Mine." "One day all enemies shall be subdued unto Me, and all knees shall bow before Me!" That is the Sovereignty of the Messiah, which the prophet once foretold; which the Nazarene claimed; which He initially demonstrated in the performance of miracles; which is described by His apostles, and which the church of Christ confesses on the authority of the apostles, undivided but delegated; or rather, assumed to be returned eventually. For when once that perfect harmony breaks through, the Sovereignty will be transmitted from the Messiah to God Himself, Who will then be "all in all".

But behold now the glorious Freedom idea! That perfect and absolute Sovereignty of the sinless Messiah at the same time contains the direct denial and challenge of all absolute Sovereignty on earth in sinful man; because of the division of life into spheres, each with its own Sovereignty.

Our human life, with its material foreground, which is visible, and its spiritual background, which is invisible, obviously is neither simple nor uniform, but forms an infinitely structured organism. It is so structured that the individual exists only in groups, and the whole can reveal itself only in those groups. One may refer to the parts of this one great instrument as wheels, spring-driven on their own axles, or call them spheres, each filled with its own exciting life-spirit -- the name or figure is unimportant -- provided that one acknowledges that, as innumerable as the constellations in the firmament, various circles exist in this life, whose circumference is drawn with a firm radius from the center of a specific principle; the apostolic "every man in his own order", (1 Cor. 15:23). Even as one speaks of a "moral world", a "scientific world", a "world of commerce" and a "world of art", so one might speak with even more justification of "a circle" of the moral, "a circle" of the domestic, "a circle" of the social life, each with its own domain, and because each constitutes its own domain with its own Sovereign within the limits of that domain.

Thus there is a domain of nature, in which the Sovereign exerts power upon matter according to fixed laws. But there is also a domain of the personal, of the domestic, of the scientific, of the social, and of the ecclesiastical life; each of which obeys its own law of life, and each subject to its own head. There is a domain of thought in which no law may prevail except the law of logic. A domain of conscience where none may exercise sovereign rule except the Holy One. And finally, a domain of faith within whose limits only the individual is Sovereign, and through that faith consecrates himself with his whole being.

Now in all of these spheres or circles the cogwheels engage one another, and it is precisely because of the mutual interaction of these spheres that there is an emergence of that rich, many-sided, multi-formed human life; but in that life there is also the danger that one sphere may encroach upon the neighboring sphere; thus causing a wheel to jerk and to break cog upon cog, and interfering with the progress of the whole. Hence the reason for existence of a special sphere of authority in the Authority of the State, which must provide for these various spheres, insofar as they emerge into the visible realm, a felicitous interaction, and to keep them within the pale of justice; and which also, since one's personal life can be depressed by the group in whose midst one lives, must shield the individual from the domination of his sphere. A Sovereign who, as the Scriptures state so tersely, "establishes the throne by righteousness", whereas without righteousness it will fall and destroy itself. Thus this State Sovereignty, as the power which protects the individual and determines the mutual righteous relations of the visible spheres of life because it has the right to command and to compel, rises far above all of these. But it does not obtain *within* any of these spheres. There another authority rules, an authority which, without any effort of its own, descends from God, and which it does not confer but acknowledges. And even in defining justice in connection with the mutual relations of these spheres, this State Sovereign may not use his own will or choice as a criterion, but he is bound by the choice of a Higher Will, as expressed by the nature and *raison d'etre* [reason for being; purpose] of these spheres. He must make the wheels to turn as they are destined to turn. Not to oppress life nor to bind freedom, but to make possible a free exercise of life for and in each of these spheres, is not this a beckoning ideal for every noble State Sovereign?

Thus these two credos stand in clear-cut opposition to each other.

He whose life proceeds from the Revelational sphere (and who live consistently in that sphere) confesses, as a matter of course, that all Sovereignty rests in God, and therefore can proceed only from Him; that this Sovereignty of God has been conferred upon the man-Messiah in the absolute sense and undivided; and that therefore man's freedom is safe in the hands of this Son of Man, anointed to be Sovereign, because, along with the State, every other sphere of life knows that supremacy derived from Him, i.e., it possesses sphere sovereignty.

On the other hand, those who do not perceive the reality of such a special revelational sphere and therefore deny it, insist that there must be absolute separation between the problem of Sovereignty and the problem of faith; they consequently assert that any Sovereignty, other than that of the State, is unthinkable; they therefore zealously promote the embodiment of the Sovereignty idea, in its purest sense, in the Supreme State; and accordingly they cannot grant to other life spheres a more generous freedom than that which is permitted or granted by the State.

I called these pronouncements Credos about Sovereignty; life convictions, not systems, because the chasm which separates them is not to be found in a different arrangement of thought but in a recognition or denial of the facts of life. For us, whose life proceeds from Revelation, that Messiah lives, that Christ reigns, and as Sovereign He is seated upon the throne of God's power more actually than you are seated here. Conversely, he who does not confess this must contest it as an annoying self-deception which stands in the way of the people's development; a fatal dogma; a senseless vision! Thus they are diametrically opposed confessions, which were indeed concealed aside again and again behind a series of hybrid systems; mixtures of more of this and less of that or perhaps an equal amount of each. But as principial credos, from which this sallowness derived its basic tint, they always angrily broke through this unprincipled play during critical times, and with raised visor were ready to resist and to offer combat, as the only two gigantic antitheses which rend life at its root, and are therefore deserving of one's risking his life while he is disturbing another's life.

"Sphere Sovereignty" defending itself against "State Sovereignty" -- that is the course of world history, prior to the proclamation of the Messianic Sovereignty, For the Royal Child of Bethlehem does indeed cover that "Sphere Sovereignty" with His shield, but He did not create it. It existed of old. It was an essential part of the order of creation; in the plan of human life; it was there before State Sovereignty came into existence. But after it appeared that State Sovereignty suspected Sphere Sovereignty of being its permanent adversary, and within those spheres the power to resist was dissipated by the violation of their own rule of life, i.e., by sin. Thus ancient history presents to our view among all peoples the shameful spectacle that, after persevering, and sometimes heroic struggle, freedom in one's own sphere perishes, and the power of the State, turning into Caesarism, gains the upper hand. Socrates, drinking the poison cup; Brutus, plunging the dagger into Caesar's heart; the Galileans, whose blood Pilate mingled with their sacrifices; all of these are the wild, heroic paroxysms of a free organic life, which finally collapses under the iron fist of that Caesarism. When the age of antiquity draws to a close there is no more freedom; no nations; no spheres. All has become one sphere, one world-empire under one Sovereign State. And only the intoxication of an emasculating opulence served a humanity sunk in ignominy to remove the offense of that ignominy from its heart.

It was Jesus the Nazarene who then, by superhuman power, the power of faith, again created within the "all of one kind" in the iron ring a free sphere and within that sphere a free Sovereignty. God in the heart, one with God, Himself God, He resisted Caesar, broke down the iron gates, and posited the sovereignty of faith as the basis upon which all Sphere Sovereignty rests. Neither Pharisee nor disciple understood that, aside from the salvation of the elect, His "Finished" also included a liberation of the world, a world of freedoms. But Jesus discovered it. Hence the *Basileus* [Sovereign] on His cross. He appeared as Sovereign. He contended with the intruding "Prince of this world" for the ruling power over that world, as its Sovereign. And His followers had hardly formed their own sphere before they also collided with State Sovereignty. They succumbed. Their blood flowed. But the sovereign principle of faith of Jesus cannot be washed away with their blood. Deus Christus or Divus Augustus [Christ is God or Augustus is divine] will be the shibboleth that will determine the fate of the world. And Christ triumphs, and Caesar topples and all the liberated nations again appear with their own kings, and within the dominion of those kings with their own spheres, and in those spheres their own freedoms. That was the beginning of that glorious life, crowned with knights' honor, and in an increasingly rich organism of guilds, orders, and free communion exhibiting all the energy and all the glory that are part of sphere sovereignty.

That was more apparent in our beloved fatherland than else-where. It seemed that the land, divided into polder [low-lying farmland] spheres, unitedly could defend Sphere Sovereignty against State Sovereignty. Philip [III of Spain] experienced that, when the singers of the Souter songs [Psalms] and the leaders of the [illegal] hedge [or field] preaching clashed with State Sovereignty. It was experienced also in the following century by the Stuarts [British dynasty] and the Bourbons [French dynasty], when the immortal naval hero whose mausoleum we see before us, our great [Michiel Adriaenszoon] De Ruyter, resisted the rising royalism of Charles [II of Spain] and Louis [XIV of France] on all seas and broke it on all shores. "I am, next to God, the skipper of my ship!" expressed the inextinguishable sense of freedom that inspired him and the entire phalanx of our naval heroes [the Sea Beggars], and in seaman's language proclaimed on all seas the legal term "Sovereign in my own sphere".

But alas, ere a century had passed, our nation suffered a de-cline; Holland sank away into sin; and the last strong bulwark of freedom remaining on Europe's mainland succumbed with our republic. Thus the current of royalism increased. It began to tread upon the lands, to trample upon the peoples, and to torment the nations, until finally in the most inflammable of those nations the fire of revenge was kindled, passions flared, and the principial Revolution took the crowned head of the Sovereign and placed the crown upon a sovereign people. A terrifying event, born of thirst for freedom but also of hatred for the Messiah, and which only served to increase the harassment of freedom! For the Sovereign of that one balloting day, through the medium of that ballot box, involuntarily placed himself or the next day under absolute guardianship; first of the Jacobins, then of the Napoleonic Caesar, and the appealing ideal of the state hurriedly realized in France; eventually advocated as just and "vernunftmässig" [rational] by Germany's group of philosophers.

Thus freedom was again cast down in disgrace, and once more a single Sovereignty threatened to swallow all other Sovereignties. What saved the day at that time? No, not the restoration spirit of the Congress of Vienna. Not the monarch idolization of [Karl Ludwig] Von Haller and [Joseph] De Maistre. Not the historical school, which rather stifled every higher principle by reason of its physiological views. Nor even the pseudo-constitutional system with its "roi fainéant" [do-nothing king, i.e., a mere titular monarch] and its tyrannizing factions. It was the Messiah, the Sovereign seated at God's right hand, who by means of the most marvelous Revival [the Calvinistic *Réveil*, or awakening of the early 1800s] that ever awakened those nations again sent among those nations a spirit of grace, prayer, and faith. For thus there came again into existence a sphere all its own in which a Sovereign other than an earthly power was worshiped. A sphere which reckoned with the soul; which practiced mercy; which inspired the states "not as statesmen but as confessors of the Evangel" [gospel]. Not by political manipulation but by moral strength there was thus born in the soul a hope of the nations; and thus, also in our fatherland, that part of the people that pays homage to the Messiah, the *pars Christiana* [Christian part], became a national party, not by design, not to rule, but to serve. Not a faction, i.e., a conceived deliberate group; not a fraction, i.e., a piece broken off; but a people's party, i.e., people's portion, according to the in *partes dilabi*, "falling apart in segments", of that which constitutes the whole. All of this in order that, if possible, by means of this temporary dividing the whole, the glorious people's unity may again be inspired to seek a higher ideal. [Willem] Bilderdijk drew the outline of that sphere, when he uprooted the People's Sovereignty with the axe of his song; [Isaac] Da Costa sounded the keynote with his hymn to the Sovereign Messiah; and finally [Guillaume] Groen van Prinsterer wrote the constitutional credo, with his eloquent formula "Sphere Sovereignty". And by virtue of this principle descended from God there has been, for a period of thirty years, a wrestling upon our knees, a seeking of those that strayed away, and evangelization with the "passion des âmes" [passion of souls]. In keeping with that principle, one institution after another has arisen as a house of mercy, to adorn our heritage. For the sake of that principle men have been reviled, rest has been renounced, and gold has been offered upon the altar. It has been zealously preached to the people; prayer has been offered before the throne; its cause has been pleaded in the courts. "Sphere Sovereignty, under Jesus' sovereign supremacy!" This is what united this sphere of the brethren, in spite of other things that might have separated them. Hence a restless exertion, which steeled our little strength; a rowing against the stream, which stimulated our courage; a *pressa uberior* [abounding under pressure], which caused the compressed spring to recoil without fail. And thus a gradual growing in spontaneity above our compatriots, whose superiority in many other respects we humbly acknowledge.

Thus we contended for the indivisibility of sovereign authority. For the States General [Parliament or Congress] as next to and jointly with, not in or under the government. Thus we maintained, not a deterring theory, but God's sovereign vengeance, upon him who dared to shed man's blood. Thus our protest was raised against compulsory inoculation [vaccination] of our children. Thus we prophesied concerning the liberation of the Church. And thus, finally, our fight was concentrated in the fight about the public school, when in that school the sovereignty of conscience, the sovereignty of the family sphere, the sovereignty of the pedagogical sphere, and the sovereignty of the spiritual sphere were threatened. And because a principle, sowing seed according to its kind, cannot rest until all its germs [seeds] are budding in scientifically ordered coherence and a national party taking a stand for such a principle may not desist ere it has cultivated the fruit of science from the root of faith, and because such an encompassing science can be cultivated only in a school with University aspirations, -- it had to come; it had to come with logical consistency, urged by a driving inner force, to what has today become a reality, namely the launching of this indeed small and unseaworthy vessel, but which, chartered under the Sovereignty of King Jesus, expects to display in all ports of learning its flag "Sphere Sovereignty".

II. Sphere Sovereignty's Scientific Purpose

"Sphere Sovereignty" is also to be presented as the emblem of our scientific purposes. I would also view this from the practical side. No abstract scholastic dryness, but adherence to principle, depth of insight, clarity of judgment, in one word, sanctified intellectual power, as a power to resist superior power that would limit the freedom in and of our human life. Do not forget that every State power is inclined to look upon freedom with suspicion. The various spheres of life cannot do without the State sphere, for even as space cannot limit space, so in the visible sense one sphere cannot limit the other, unless the State limits their boundaries by law. The State is the sphere of spheres which encloses our human life in an encompassing whole, wherefore (not for its own benefit but for the benefit of all spheres) it seeks to strengthen its arm, and with that outstretched arm opposes and attempts to break every aspiration of those spheres toward expansion. Even now, observe the signs of the times. Did not [Theodor] Mommsen, in the vigorous image of Caesar that he presented, indicate that the return to the imperialistic line drawn by that Caesar would be the directive for the statesmen's wisdom of our century? Does Germany's chancellor [Otto von Bismarck] present a freedom-loving figure to you? Was it the man [Napoleon III of France] who suffered such inexpressibly deep humiliation at Sedan at the hands of that chancellor? Freedom-loving or tyrannical, what is your impression of the people's tribune that has replaced the man of Sedan in France's capital city in influencing the people?

And that had to be, both as a means of discipline and as a cure for the cowardly and emasculated nations which made possible this assault upon their freedom because of the atrophy of their moral resilience. The State happens to be the supreme power on earth. There is no earthly power above the State that can compel the Sovereign to administer justice. Therefore, whether it be because of a base lust for power or a noble solicitude for the common good, every State will eventually drive the iron band so tightly around the [barrel] staves as the elasticity of the staves permits. In the final analysis therefore it depends upon the life spheres themselves whether they will blossom in an air of freedom or groan under the yoke of the State. If they possess moral resilience they cannot be pushed; they will not permit themselves to be put in a straitjacket; but servility forfeits even the right to complain when it is shackled. But here is the sore spot; the threat to freedom by sin within the sphere is equally as strong as the threat by State power at its boundaries. When a man wants to drive the iron band around the staves, he lights a fire within the circle of staves, and the fire within causes the staves to shrink more than the hammer blows from without. Thus it is with our freedoms. Within every life sphere a flame of passion is smoldering and smoking; the sparks of sin leap up, and that unholy fire undermines the moral vitality, weakens the resiliency in every sphere, and eventually causes the toughest staves to shrink. In every successful assault upon freedom the State can therefore be only an accomplice; the chief culprit is the citizen, forgetful of his duty, devoid of the power of personal initiative, because his moral vigor was weakened in a life of sin and sensual pleasures. Among a people sound in its national core, and living a sound life in its various spheres, no State can wrest justice without experiencing the people's strong moral opposition, under God. It was only when discipline departed, opulence entered, and sin became brazen, that theory was able to bend that which was weakened, and Napoleon could crush that which was moldering. And if God had not poured vigor into those lifeless life spheres, again and again, also by means of depression, in order to change atoms into dynamos (as a new philosophy has it), the last sphere would long since have been broken down, and the only remains of freedom would be the "sic transit" [thus passes away] on its tomb.

Among the means of defense which God granted to more enlightened peoples to maintain their freedoms we also find science or learning. Among the Holy Spirit's interpreters the man of Tarsus [the Apostle Paul] stood out as the scientifically trained, and [Martin] Luther drew his freedom of the Reformation not from the meditative John, nor from the practical James, but from the Pauline treasure chest. I realize that learning could also betray freedom, and indeed did betray it more than once, but that was in spite of, and not by virtue of, its sacred mission. Taken in its real form, God sent it to us as an angel of light. For is it not the lack of clear consciousness that robs the lunatic, the idiot, and the drunkard of his human aspect? And to come to a clear consciousness, not only of self, but also of that which exists outside of self, is that not the essence of science? God's reflection concerning His thoughts for, about, and in us? The life consciousness not only of an individual, but of humanity of all ages! To be able to contemplate that which is, and thus to summarize in our understanding that which is reflected in our consciousness, is God's gracious arrangement for our human existence. To possess wisdom is a divine trait in our being. Indeed, the power of wisdom and science extends so far that the course of things usually is not according to reality, but according to how man imagines that reality. Who would say that ideas are unimportant? Those ideas shape public opinion; those opinions form the sense of justice; and according to that sense the current of spiritual life is thawed out or congealed. Consequently, one who expects his principles to exert an influence cannot continue to float in an atmosphere of feeling; does not advance with fancy; indeed only arrives at the half-way point with his confession; and only obtains a hold on the public if he attained power also in the world of thought, and if he was able to transfer his inner urge, the "Deus in nobis" [God in us], from what he senses to what he knows.

Provided, and to that I cling tenaciously, that this science remains "Sovereign in its own sphere", and does not degenerate under State or Church guardianship.

Science, too, creates its own life sphere, in which Truth is Sovereign, and under no circumstances may violation of its vital law be tolerated. To do so would not only dishonor science, but would also be sin before God. Our consciousness is as a mirror within us, in which images are reflected from three worlds: the world around us, the world of our own being, and the invisible world of the spirits. Reason demands that: 1) each of these worlds be permitted to reflect those images according to their own nature, i.e., observation and perception; 2) to catch the reflections with a clear eye, i.e., to view those images until we understand them; 3) to make a harmonious summary of that which our eye has caught, i.e., to understand what we have seen in its coherence, as being necessary and beautiful. No contemplation therefore, but reflection in us. Science that produces wisdom. From life for life, ending in adoration of the only wise God!

[Baruch] Spinoza grasped the Sovereignty of science in its own sphere, and therefore our admiration for Spinoza's character is as great as our disapproval of the insipid [Desiderius] Erasmus, measured by moral standards. In the case of Spinoza, both organ and perception were faulty, wherefore his conclusion was necessarily false. But the fact that, seeing what he saw and as he saw it, he declined steadfastly to lend his name to a violation of Sovereignty of science in its own sphere, that is not censurable for a true Reformed person, but he considers it far superior to the wavering instability which tempted many, who knew what Spinoza never knew; to agree to an unprincipled compromise. We must therefore insist that the Church of Jesus Christ may never force its supremacy upon science. At the risk of suffering at the hands of science, the church must urge that science never become a slave, but maintain the Sovereignty which is its due in its own sphere, and live by the grace of God. There is indeed a satanic danger that some will degenerate into devils of pride, and will tempt science to arrogate unto itself that which is outside of its sphere. However, a high steeple cannot be scaled without facing the danger of a serious fall, and further, what we stated about the tyranny of the State can also be applied to the tyranny of science; it cannot arise unless the church declines spiritually; and also, when there is a spiritual awakening in the church it will urge science, which chastised it in God's Name, back to its own precise confines.

Not wholly, but approximately the same may be said of the State. Not wholly, for also in the sphere of science, when that science assumes the form of a visible organism in the schools, the State remains the absolute master planner who has been given the power to define its rightful sphere. But even that State power, ere it crosses the boundary into the sphere of science, will differentially unloose the latchet of its shoes, and lay aside a sovereignty which would not be seemly on that terrain. Science as servant of the State, such as the Ghibellines played off against the Guelphs [rival factions in northern Italy during the late-11th and early 12th centuries] ; France's bureaucracy misused in its attempt to dominate the people; and German reaction sought to create for itself by the shame of Göttingen; this is the prostituted self-debasement which forfeits every valid claim to moral influence. But even though, as in our government circles, the State is animated by a more noble nature, and though science, as in our country, is too proud to stoop, nevertheless that science will prosper and flourish only if, also in the life of the University, it will again base itself upon its own root, and growing into a life of its own will outgrow State guardianship. Thus the schools of the prophets in Israel and the schools of the Chokhmah in Jerusalem stood independent in the center of the nation. Thus, independent, the schools of the ancient Greek philosophers and their imitators in Rome took their stand. Thus, independent, the schools of the first Christian scholars appeared at one time. And equally independent were the ancient Universities of Bologna and Paris. Not as the shaping of a cadre of the State into which to pour knowledge, but knowledge which manifested itself in life, and created its own image in that life. It was that independent image which enabled the University to be active in the liberation of the Reformation, and it was not until the close of the previous century that this independent cadre was conjured into a "branch of the State" when the new-fashioned University permitted itself to be attached as an organ of the State.

This came about, not because of personal arbitrariness, but because of the press of events; because of the innervation of the nations; and it would border on the absurd to demand that the State would now suddenly relinquish its hold on the University world. At present the masses display too little desire for science; there is too little generosity on the part of the wealthy; and too little energy in the circle of graduates to make such an attempt. For the present the State must continue its support, provided, and this we insist, there is a striving in the direction of liberation, and science again grasps "Sphere sovereignty" as its ideal.

Is it unscientific, therefore, that our School should venture to take its first timid step in that better direction? At the State university the scale of equity is weighed down by so many burdens. We cannot repeat often enough that money creates power for the one who gives, and over the one who receives. Hence the arts (except music) can never elevate the people's freedom permanently because of their need of gold. Who can gauge the influence which, because of those State funds, has been wrought upon the destiny of our nation and the course of science by one single appointment such as that of [Johan Rudolph] Thorbecke, [Willem Albert] Scholten, or [Cornelius Willem] Opzoomer? Where is the spiritual criterion that can guide the State in making its influential choice for the higher, most critical sciences? Moreover, to compel the Jew and the Roman Catholic to contribute to the support of a theological faculty, which in reality is and must be Protestant, would seem to be not in keeping with a sense of justice. And if the law of the land, as we heard earlier, includes our free, unburdened institution in the sphere of justice, is there not then a glorious prophecy for science and life in a University supported by the people?

Indeed, here is a group which was given the sobriquet [nickname] of obscurantists less than thirty years ago, and which is now exhausting its strength in the interest of the cause of learning! The least esteemed of the "non-thinking" segment of the nation, who come running from the plow and the shop to gather funds for a University. Elsewhere there is a zeal for progress to come from above; science is to be brought to the people. But is not this something superior, a group of people which is willing to curtail its pleasures in order that science may blossom? Is there a more practical solution to the problem of combining science and life? Is it not essential that scientists who subsist on funds supplied by the people grow together with the people, and show an aversion to all abstractions? And in addition to that, is not giving in itself a power; is not the ability to part with money a moral asset; who then will rightly value the moral capital that will accrue to our people through this costly Institution? Complaints have been made about lack of character, but what can be more helpful in forming character than such free initiative on the part of vigilant citizens? And if elsewhere the wheel of the University should turn by the compelling power of the recipients and the readiness of the paymasters, we will not be envious; for if, in our case, it is the struggle for life, it is precisely in that struggle that the power of glorious devotion is generated. In the money entrusted to us there is a value other and greater than the intrinsic worth of the metal; prayer, and love, and sweat adhere to the gold which flows into our coffers.

III. SPHere Sovereignty's Reformed Character

We have seen that "Sphere Sovereignty" was the stimulus that gave birth to our Institution; it was frankly stated that "Sphere Sovereignty" is also among us the royal condition for the blossoming of all science. It now remains for me to plead for a disputed demand, namely that we be granted "Sphere Sovereignty" for our principle, that is the Reformed principle. However, when I mention that name, I would immediately refute a chronic misunderstanding, and dispel every suspicion that we interpret Reformed as being anything other or less than the real, true Christianity. Even as the merchant speaks of net weight, the minter of fine gold, the silversmith of hallmark, the Scripture of precious spikenard, and a certain newspaper in the city on the Spaarne calls itself the upright, so we also if we wished to be eccentric, could speak of a "net" Christianity, a "fine" Christianity, a "precious" Christianity, a Christianity carrying a "hallmark"; but we will pass by such strange terms, and rather speak, according to usage and the demands of history, of Reformed, in order that we may draw a sharp distinction between imitation, adulterated, stunted, and the Christianity that is Scriptural. To speak merely of "Christian" is meaningless, for that could also be "Roman Catholic" or "Remonstrant" [Arminian]. None of the modernists have yet abandoned the "Christian name". Has it not been observed that men who consider it an honor to deny the existence of God displayed the false banner "Christian" over the entrance of a de-Christianized school, and that this was done in a session of the States General [Parliament or Congress]? Something must be added. We cannot escape the confusion of tongues at a lesser cost. And since also in the spiritual realm Sphere Sovereignty is applicable, and it is therefore not the prerogative of the individual to coin names for principles or to define those principles, but that right is reserved for the directing organ which is the bearer of historic life in that sphere, it was not for us to choose another name. Neither were we authorized to confess our principles arbitrarily, but we had to present the "Reformed name" which we bore as sons of the Netherlands Reformation, and to comprehend in that name not what we pleased but the church's lawful judgment, namely a courageous and unconditional confession of the Canons of Dort [1619]. This does not mean that we reject our Lutheran brethren. To look down upon other Christians would be culpable. We merely ask that we be not compelled to exchange that which we consider finer for something less fine, and that we be permitted to rebuild, according to the pure Reformed style, the Reformed temple which had fallen into ruin.

In this discourse I also contended for this, and therefore placed God's Sovereignty in the foreground, according to the demands of Scripture and [John] Calvin's teaching, because this sovereignty stimulates life to its roots, and overcomes all fear of men and of Satan himself. And if anyone should ask whether this Sphere Sovereignty is derived from the heart of the Scriptures and from the treasure of Reformed life, I would beg of him first to fathom the depths of the organic principle of faith of the Scriptures, further to take note of Hebron's tribal law for David's coronation; to notice Elijah's resistance to Ahab's tyranny; the refusal of the disciples to yield to Jerusalem's police regulations; and not least, to listen to their Lord's maxim concerning what is God's and what is Caesar's. And touching upon Reformed life, do you not know Calvin's "magistratus inferiores" [lesser magistrates]? Is not Sphere Sovereignty the basis of the entire presbyterial church order? Did not almost all Reformed nations incline toward a confederative mode of existence? Did not the freedom of the citizens expand most luxuriantly in the Calvinist nations? And can it be denied that domestic peace, decentralization, and autonomy of municipalities are best guaranteed even now on the promises of the *issus de Calvin* [Calvin's children]?

Thus it is entirely in line with the Reformed spirit that we now ask for Sovereignty for our own principle in our own scientific sphere. We may not make a compact of neutrality with science that proceeds from another principle, and be seated at the same table. For although I do not deny that among the non-Christian authorities there exists a fear of God and of His justice, a fear which Calvin honored even in the case of pagan tyrants, yet such a pious trait is nothing more than the foundation and at most a section of wall, but without roof or windows. Or, to present a clearer picture, of what use is an erected tower which lacks the spire, and therefore the carillon [bells], the clock, and the weathervane, in short everything for which it was built? More acceptable would be that other proposal, for a large State academy, for which the authorities would furnish nothing but auditoriums equipped with lecterns and also musea [galleries] and laboratories, in which every scholar had the right to appear, and every sphere the right to place its scholars. It would be a sort of Central Station, where all lines would converge, but each with its own direction and administration. But even then the royal right of every principle to have its own Sphere Sovereignty would be mutually violated. Does not history teach that science assumed a totally different form in every sphere of life that was endowed with its own principle? For there has existed a Greek science, an Arabic science, a Scholastic science, and, although we have no kinship with them, each in its own sphere was duly considered and well thought out by giant intellects, and none of us could stand in their shadow. Likewise, Catholic and non-Roman-Catholic Universities. The succession of philosophers who appeared with and after [Immanuel] Kant established schools of science which, depending upon whether they stressed the subjective or the objective, were mutually exclusive. How could one promote a marriage between a Monist and an Atomist? Indeed, the power of a principle is so compelling and dominating that it is generally conceded that Hegel's intellectual power was able to produce individual systems for every area --theological, juridical, physical, etc., so that anyone studying criminal law in Hegel's school and civil law in [Johann Friedrich] Herbart's school would find his sense of justice totally confused.

And if this impossibility of cooperation in the weaving of a garment is apparent when there is a difference in thought principle, how much more imperative is the necessity of Sphere Sovereignty in the case of a life principle! As indicated by [Johann Gottlieb] Fichte's example, if only a thought principle is involved it is possible to return to what was originally rejected. But that cannot be done in the case of a life principle. That is rooted in facts. Or, to put it more strongly, in a living person. In a person whose appearance precipitated a world crisis. For if you interrogate this living person, this Christ, or His authoritative interpreters, what do you learn? Does that Rabbi in Nazareth [Jesus] state that his science is wedded to that of those earthly sages? Do the apostles tell you that a postgraduate course at Jerusalem or Athens will gradually and naturally lead to His higher knowledge? No, the reverse is true. That rabbi will impress upon you that His treasure of wisdom had been hidden from the wise and prudent, and revealed to babes. And the scientifically trained Paul draws a gulf between his earlier acquired science and the life principle that has since been implanted, a gulf so wide, so deep, and so impassable that he terms the thought sphere of the one foolishness, and the life sphere of the other wisdom. Shall we then pretend that we can cultivate on one root that which, according to Jesus' divine self-consciousness, is rooted differently? We shall not attempt it, Gentlemen! Rather, considering that a principle is the beginning of something, and therefore one's distinct principle produces something distinct, we shall maintain a distinct Sphere Sovereignty for our principle, and another for that of our opponents, in the entire sphere of thought. That is to say, even as they, according to their principle and the method suited to that principle, erect a house of science which sparkles, but does not tempt us, so also will we, from the root of our principle, and according to the method which fits our principle, permit a trunk to grow whose branches, leaves, and blossoms are nourished by its distinct life sap. We claim to have discovered something which our opponents label as self-deception. So be it; to be considered fools for that reason is as needful for us as we are unable to refrain from saying with the poet of Proverbs: "that the godless of our age do not understand wisdom." We do not say that he is inferior to us in knowledge. He may be our superior in that respect. But we do say, with Proverbs, that he lacks wisdom because he denies that which is for us an assured fact in Christ, and also states that he has not found in his soul what we consciously grasped in our soul. Faith in God's Word, objectively infallible in the Scriptures, and subjectively offered to us by the Holy Spirit, behold the line of demarcation. This does not mean that the knowledge of others is based upon intellectual certainty, and ours only upon faith. For all knowledge proceeds from faith of one or another. One leans upon God, proceeds from one's ego, or holds to one's ideal. The man does not exist who believes nothing. At least, one who had no facts to begin with could not find even a starting point for his thinking; and how can the man whose thinking lacks every starting point ever investigate anything scientifically?

Indeed, we purpose therefore to build alongside of what others built, without anything in common except the outdoors, the view from the windows, and a press which, like a mail carrier, maintains the communion of thought. For we also acknowledge that the mutual struggle between thoughts is possible and necessary, but never concerning anything except starting point and direction. When once these have been defined your line is drawn, provided you draw a straight line, and depending upon whether you are to the right or the left of that line your views will not coincide, and any argument that might be advanced will lack the power of conviction. Every organical thinker will rightly ridicule all atomic pretension that all growing persons must think through every system and search through every confession, and thereafter choose what he considers best for him. Nobody can or will do that, because neither time nor intellectual power is available for it. And only the unwise can fancy that he did it or believe that others did it, if he himself does not understand science. Such sampling of all systems merely feeds superficiality, ruins thinking, spoils character, and makes the brain unfit for more solid labor. Believe me, not a cursory glance at all houses, but a careful examination of one well-built house from basement to attic will enhance one's knowledge of building construction.

Our science will therefore not be "free" in the sense of "detached from its principles". That would be the freedom of a fish on dry land, of a flower uprooted from the soil, or if you will, a Drents [someone from the northwest province of Drenthe] day-laborer taken from the environment of his village and suddenly set down in "Fleet Street" or on the "Strand". Sternly and inexorably we bind ourselves in our own house to a definite rule of life, being convinced that domestic life flourishes best when controlled by definite rules. For the most generous freedom in the realm of science is this, that the door will be opened for those who would leave; that no outsider will enter your house to lord it over you; but also, that everyone can build freely on the foundation of his own method, and the results which he produced serving as the cornice [capstone].

Finally, if you ask whether we desire this individual scientific development not only for theology, but for all disciplines, and if possibly you can scarcely control a smile when you hear scoffing references to "Christian medicine" and "Christian logic" -- hear our reply to that objection.

Or do you think that we, confessing God's revelation as it was again reformed after the deformation, as the starting point of our striving, would limit drawing from that source to the theologians, and that physicians, jurists, and philologists would scorn this fountainhead? Do you feel that there exists a science, worthy of the name, whose professional knowledge is separated from others in pigeonholes? Why speak of a medical faculty! It is not a sick mammal that medical science seeks to benefit hygienically, but a man created after God's image. Judge for yourselves, then, whether depending upon your view of that man as a moral being, with a higher destiny for soul and body, bound to God's Word, or not so viewing him, whether you ought to tell him of approaching death or to keep it from him; whether you ought to recommend or advise against anesthesia for a woman in travail; whether you ought to compel vaccination or leave it to a person's free choice; whether you ought to advise passionate youth as to self-control or indulgence; whether you shall curse the fertility of the mother with Malthus[ianism] or bless it with the Scriptures; whether you must guide the mentally deranged psychically or anesthetize him physically; in short, whether you condone cremation; permit vivisection unconditionally; and whether you would halt the spread of syphilitic poison in society, at the cost of violating authority and human dignity by means of the most detestable of all medical examinations.

What shall I say of the study of law? This depends upon whether one sees man as a self-developing product of nature or as a sinner worthy of condemnation; whether one sees justice as a functionally developing natural organ or as a treasure coming down to us from God and bound to His Word; whether there was not another purpose in choosing criminal law, and another guideline in choosing international law. If, aside from science, the Christian conscience shows resistance to the prevailing political economy, to the current business practices, and to the rapacious nature of social relationships; if in civil life our Christian people urge a return to decentralization by way of "Sphere Sovereignty"; and if [as allowed by] constitutional law there appear three [independent] "Christian schools" [for every one non-Christian school]; is it possible then to think of one chair in the faculty of law that would not be harmed by these contrasting principles?

I will readily grant you that, if our faculty of the natural sciences would strictly limit itself to measuring and weighing, the wedge of principle could not enter its doors. But who would do that? Which physicist operates without hypotheses? What man who practices his science as a man and not as a measuring device does not view what he sees through subjective lenses, and does not add by dotted line the invisible part of the circle, always according to subjective opinion? The man who figures the cost of the printed paper and the drops of ink that were used in printing, is that man able to assess the value of the book that you published, your pamphlet, or your book of songs in a higher sense? Is the value of the most beautiful piece of embroidery to be rated according to the cost of a few strands of silk? Or, if you prefer, is not all of creation open before the eyes of the natural scientist, like one enchanting painting, and is the value and beauty of that work of art to be judged by the gold frame around it, the yards of canvas under it, and the pounds of paint on it?

And what shall I say about the faculty of literature? Of course, learning the "reading" of words and "declension" of words has nothing to do with being for or against the Messiah.

But if I, continuing, unlock the doors of Hellas' palace of art, or enter Rome's world of power, does it not concern you whether I recall the spirit of those nations in order to banish the spirit of Christ, or place them in subjection to the spirit of Christ, both according to human and divine evaluation? Does not the study of Semitic languages take on another aspect, depending upon whether I view Israel as the people of the absolute revelation, or merely as a people with a genius for piety? Does philosophy remain the same, whether it pursues the "ideal being" or joins us in confessing the Christ as the ideal "made flesh"? Will world history arrive at the same result, regardless whether one identifies the cross with Socrates' cup of poison or views it as the central point of all history? And finally, will the history of the fatherland kindle the same fire in the heart of youth, regardless whether it is unfolded by [Robert Jacobus] Fruin or [Willem Jan Frans] Nuyens or Groen van Prinsterer (oh that he were still alive) in all its heroic beauty?

How could it be otherwise? Man as a fallen sinner, contrasted with man as a self-developing product of nature, will appear again as "the subject that thinks" or "the object that prompts one to think", in every faculty, every science, and with every research worker. Oh, there is not one part of our world of thought that can be hermetically separated from the other parts; and there is not a square inch in the whole domain of our human life of which Christ, Who is Sovereign of all, does not cry: "Mine!"

Now, we declare that we have heard that cry, and only in response to that cry have we approached this task which surpasses our human strength. We had heard brethren complain about their tragic impotence. Because their learning did not fit their principle and left them defenseless, they could not plead their principle with the power commensurate with the glory of that principle. We had heard the sighs of our Christian people who, in the shame of their self-abasement, again learned to pray for captains to lead them, for shepherds to tend them, and for prophets to inspire them. We realized that the glory of the Christ may not thus remain trodden under scoffers' feet. As surely as we adored Him with the love of our souls we must again build in His Name. And it was of no avail to look upon our little power or the superior might of our opponents, or the preposterousness of such a daring attempt. The fire continued to burn in our bones. There was One, mightier than we, Who urged and spurred us on. We could not rest. In spite of ourselves we had to go forward. Even the fact that some of our brethren, advising against building at this time, preferred living in with Humanism, was a painful source of shame, but increased the inner urge, because the hesitation of such men was an increasingly strong threat to the future of our life principle.

Thus our small School came upon the scene, embarrassed to the point of blushing with the name "University"; poor in funds; not well supplied with scientific man-power, and lacking, rather than receiving men's favor. What will be its course, how long its life? Oh, the thousand questions relative to its future cannot crowd your thoughts and misgivings more strongly than they have raged in this heart! Only by keeping our sacred principle in view did our weary head rise from the waters after every wave that engulfed us. If this cause be not of the Mighty One of Jacob, how can it endure? For I do not exaggerate, what we are venturing in the establishment of this School runs contrary to all that is called great, counter to a world of scholars, counter to an entire century, a century of great charm. Therefore, feel free to look down as low as your inner self deems proper upon our persons, our strength, our academic significance. "To esteem God as everything and man as nothing" is the Calvinist credo that gives you the full right to do so. I would only ask this one thing: though you may be our fiercest opponent, do not withhold the tribute of your respect from the enthusiasm that inspires us. For that confession from which we swept the dust was at one time the soul's cry of a downtrodden nation; those Scriptures before whose authority we bow have in the past, as God's infallible witness, comforted the sorrowing of your own generations; and was not that Christ, Whose Name we honor in this institution, the Inspirer, the Adored one of your own fathers? Therefore, even if we suppose, in line with your credo and in accordance with what has been written in the study and echoed in the market-place, that the Scriptures are finished and Christianity is outmoded, even then I ask: is Christianity, also in your view, historically not too imposing, too majestic, too sacred, to collapse ignominiously and to fall without honor? Or does *noblesse oblige* no longer exist? And could we permit a banner which we brought from Golgotha to fall into the hands of the enemy so long as the uttermost were left untried, so long as a single arrow remained unshot, and so long as a bodyguard, however small, of Him who crowned by Golgotha, remains in this land of our inheritance?

To that question -- and this is my final word, Gentlemen -- to that question a "*Never*, by God!" resounded in our soul. Out of the "Never" this Institution was born. And upon that "Never", as an oath of allegiance to a higher principle, I ask for an echo, may it be an Amen, from every patriotic heart!

Closing Prayer

We thank Thee, our Father Who art in heaven, Source of all truth, Fountain of all true knowledge and wisdom! The creature, straying away from Thee, finds nothing but darkness, nothing but weariness, nothing but distress of the soul. But near Thee, bathing in Thy life, the light surrounds us; strength throbs in our veins, and the freedom of faith unfolds in blessed rapture. Adorable and eternal Majesty, look with favor upon this Institution. May all its gold, its strength, its wisdom come from Thee. May it never swear by a lesser, by another than Thy Holy Word. And Thou Who dost try our reins, O Judge also of our nation and of the schools of learning, wilt Thou Thyself break down the walls of this Institution, and destroy them from before Thy Face, if ever it should purpose or will to do anything other than to glory in that sovereign and free grace which there is in the cross of the Son of Thy most tender love! Lord, Lord our God, our help be in Thy Name, and in Thy Name alone! AMEN.

www.ingramcontent.com/pod-product-compliance
Lightning Source LLC
Chambersburg PA
CBHW051336120626
46547CB00016B/2574